AMELIARAN
BRIDESM

TOLD BY ETHELBERTA MORRIS
PICTURED BY SUSAN B. PEARSE

COLLINS
PICTURE LIONS

It was the first day of the summer holidays, and Ameliaranne was feeling full of happiness. She and the five little Stigginses were playing cowboys in the garden. Mrs Stiggins was busy washing, and she was humming a little song, because it was a fine sunshiny day, good for drying.

Just then there was a click at the garden gate, and in came Nurse Bobberty, looking worried. Ameliaranne let Wee William escape from the rope she was lassooing him with, and came over to listen.

"Mrs Stiggins," said Nurse Bobberty, "do you think you could do anything for Mrs Mactavish over the way? She's in bed very poorly, and no one to look after her since her daughter went away."

Now Ameliaranne was rather frightened of Mrs Mactavish, but she stepped forward bravely when she heard Nurse Bobberty.

"I'll go and look after her," she said.

"Thank you, my dear," said Nurse Bobberty, patting her head and looking pleased.

"She won't need for anything, only some soup hotted up, and her medicine at two o'clock. Now I must go to that baby with the measles."

So Ameliaranne combed her hair and washed her face, and put her dinner and an apron in a shopping bag with coloured stripes, and off she went.

Mrs Mactavish was lying in bed, propped up with pillows.

"Well, what do you want?" she said.

"I've come to look after you, please," said Ameliaranne politely, putting on her apron.

"Oh, well," said Mrs Mactavish crossly, "since you're here, you may as well make yourself useful. Though I wish my own daughter Hetty would come home, that I do."

Ameliaranne went into the kitchen and looked around. "Needs a good turnout. I'll pretend it's my own kitchen and I'm having a spring-clean."

She swept and she scrubbed and she polished till the kitchen began to sparkle and wink.

"Now you look better," Ameliaranne said out loud, as she sat back on her heels and looked around. "But, good gracious me, it's dinner time." The kitchen clock, ticking away steadily on the mantelpiece, said just on one o'clock.

Very carefully she heated the soup.

"I'm not hungry," said Mrs Mactavish grumpily but she drank it while Ameliaranne ate her dinner downstairs.

Then Ameliaranne fetched an old snap album for Mrs Mactavish to look at.

"There's my Hetty when she was four," she said. "Now I'll never see her again. I told her that if she went to London I'd never speak to her again. She went to London a whole year ago and never a word have I heard since. She wanted to be a mannequin."

"What?" asked Ameliaranne.

"It's what they have in the big shops to show off the lovely dresses. The mannequins stroll about in them so as everybody can see how nice they look, but maybe she's starving by now. Oh, if only she'd come and see me!"

Ameliaranne walked slowly downstairs, thinking. She went through the kitchen without noticing how clean and bright it looked, and on out into the garden.

"London's a big place," she thought.

She picked some flowers, and took them into the kitchen. She found an old newspaper to spread them on, and a tall glass vase, and while she arranged them she read little bits out of the paper. It was a very old one. There was a column called 'situations vacant', and half way down was a tick in pencil just like the ticks on Ameliaranne's sums at school.

Ameliaranne's eyes began to twinkle with excitement, for this is what she read:

> A few vacancies for young ladies of good appearance to train as mannequins. Apply personally. WIGRAM and BANDOVER, Oxford Street, London.

Ameliaranne skipped round the table, and nearly shouted, "Hurry it's a clue," but she remembered just in time that Mrs Mactavish was asleep. She cut out that piece of the newspaper, and put it very carefully in her pocket, and she began to make plans.

When she went home that evening Mrs Mactavish said quite kindly,

"You're a good girl, Ameliaranne. I'm feeling better tonight."

"Sweet dreams," answered Ameliaranne. "I can't come tomorrow, but I'll try to bring you something nice at bedtime."

And she ran off quickly before Mrs Mactavish could ask her any questions.

Next day Ameliaranne got up very early before any of the little Stigginses were awake, and she dressed in her best stripey skirt and red bodice, and combed out her curls very carefully, and put on her coat and hat. Then she took all the money she had in her money-box, and crept down to the kitchen.

She left a note for her mother saying,

Am out all day on important business.
Will tell you about it tonight.
AMELIARANNE

and off she went to the station.

When Ameliaranne got to the station she went into the booking office and waited until the man who sold the tickets came and looked at her through the little window.

"Half return to London," said Ameliaranne.

"You're just in time, for there's a train in a few minutes," said the man giving her the ticket.

So Ameliaranne went out on to the platform and waited for the train to come puffing in. Then she climbed into an empty carriage.

Half way to London the train stopped at a station, and a family got in – a lady, a baby and two other children. The mother sighed.

"Are you going to London?" asked Ameliar-anne.

"We're going to my sister's for a holiday," said the lady, "and you know what it is with three children."

The tired lady sighed again, and the children stared at Ameliaranne, and sat quite still.

"Shall I nurse the baby a bit while you rest?" said Ameliaranne, as the fat baby leant forward to pull at her coat buttons.

"It's very kind of you," said the lady, and leant back in her corner gratefully.

So Ameliaranne talked to the baby and to the two children and before long the train drew into the big London station.

"Please," said Ameliaranne, as she handed the baby back. "Could you tell me how to get to Oxford Street?"

"Why, yes," said the lady. "We shall pass it in our taxi. Come along too." So Ameliaranne carried a suitcase, and climbed into the taxi with the others.

"Tell the driver where you want to go," said the lady, and Ameliaranne tapped on the glass, and shouted, "Wigram and Bandover." The taxi-man nodded, and eventually he stopped before a grand looking shop. Ameliaranne got out and said goodbye and thank you and waved her hand as the family drove away.

Then, clutching the precious piece of newspaper firmly in her hand, she pushed open the shop's heavy glass door, and walked in.

A tall, elegant lady in black came towards her, and said,

"What can I do for you, madam?" and Ameliaranne was so surprised at being called 'madam' that she could only say "Please" and hold out the bit of newspaper.

"Please sit down," said the lady, and took the piece of paper away with her.

Very soon she came back again with a short man with a shining, cheerful face.

He shook hands with Ameliaranne and said,

"You'll do, my dear. It's an extraordinary thing. You've just come in the nick of time."

"Please," began Ameliaranne again, feeling very puzzled, but the little man only said,

"This way if you please," and swept her off.

"I've found you a bridesmaid, Miss Barnstaple," he said to one of the ladies. And Miss Barnstaple smiled and took Ameliaranne by the hand and led her over to a large mirror.

"You'll have to change very quickly," she said, starting to help Ameliaranne out of her coat.

"Please," said Ameliaranne again, very firmly, "I'm looking for Miss Hetty Mactavish, and why do you want me to change my clothes?"

"Who is it that's looking for me?" said another voice, and Ameliaranne turned and saw someone dressed all in white with a veil floating down her back.

She stared at her. Was the face a little like that of the small girl in Mrs Mactavish's album?

"Are you really Hetty?" she asked.

The lady nodded.

"Oh, I am glad I've found you," said Ameliaranne, and she began to explain all about Mrs Mactavish, and how sorry she was for all she'd said, and how she longed to see Hetty again.

"Ameliaranne," said Hetty, hugging her, "we'll go home this very afternoon."

"Time you were ready," said Miss Barnstaple, briskly. Hetty began to laugh.

"I've got to show off this wedding dress, and the girl who was going to be my bridesmaid is ill. They thought you wanted a job and that you'd just do for the bridesmaid," she said.

"And so I will," said Ameliaranne, giggling.

She slipped out of her stripey skirt, and Miss Barnstaple put a misty blue gown over her head, and then fastened her into it. Her eyes were shining with happiness; her curls crinkled and gleamed as Miss Barnstaple brushed them and fixed a little crown of moonstones over her head; and her feet twinkled in soft blue dancing slippers.

"I wish Richard and Rosabel, and Jenny and Joey and Wee William could see me now," said Ameliaranne.

"It's time," said Hetty. "You must walk very slowly and grandly. But, oh, Ameliaranne, I'm so happy, I feel as if I could hop and skip!"

Out they went, down a long, thick carpet between rows of chairs. Ameliaranne held the white satin train, and walked as if she were a duchess.

There was a murmur of pleasure from the people, and someone said quite close to her,

"What a charming picture!"

Round they went, very slowly – once, twice, three times – and then back to the dressing-room, and it was all over.

Ameliaranne's frock was taken off and hung up, and she watched the other ladies showing off frocks. Velvet frocks, satin, brocaded and chiffon frocks – Ameliaranne had never seen so many clothes in her life.

"Not one you could mind a baby in," she said to herself. "I'd rather be comfortable than grand."

Hetty was soon ready to start for home. Before they left, the manager shook hands with Ameliaranne and gave her a pound note.

"For a very nice bit of work," he said.

Ameliaranne said goodbye to Miss Barnstaple and to all the ladies. They looked like ordinary people in their own coats and hats.

Ameliaranne fell asleep on the way home, but she woke up when the train stopped at the village station, and she and Hetty ran hand in hand to Mrs Mactavish's cottage. They stopped only when they reached the gate.

On the way Nurse Bobberty passed them on a bicycle, and stared hard. Suddenly she gave a beaming smile, and a wave of her hand that nearly wobbled her into the ditch.

"You go in first," said Hetty. "It's your secret." They tiptoed in, and Ameliaranne ran upstairs and knocked on Mrs Mactavish's door.

"Oh, Ameliaranne, is that you?" said Mrs Mactavish. "I was just thinking how sweet your vase of flowers looked."

"I've brought you something sweeter still," said Ameliaranne, with her eyes dancing, and then she pulled Hetty into the room, and ran off as fast as her legs would carry her.

Mrs Stiggins was ironing when she got home, and the children all came running in from the garden.

"Ameliaranne Stiggins," said her mother, putting her iron down with a bang, "whatever have you been up to?"

So Ameliaranne told them all about it.

"Well," said Mrs Stiggins, wiping her eyes with her apron as she thought of Hetty and Mrs Mactavish together again. "Well, I never heard the like!"

"And this," said Ameliaranne, giving Mrs Stiggins the pound note, "this is what they gave me for playing at dressing up."

"Hurrah for Ameliaranne," shouted all the little Stigginses, and Wee William slipped his hand into hers.

"Will you come and play weddings with me, 'Meliaranne?" he asked.

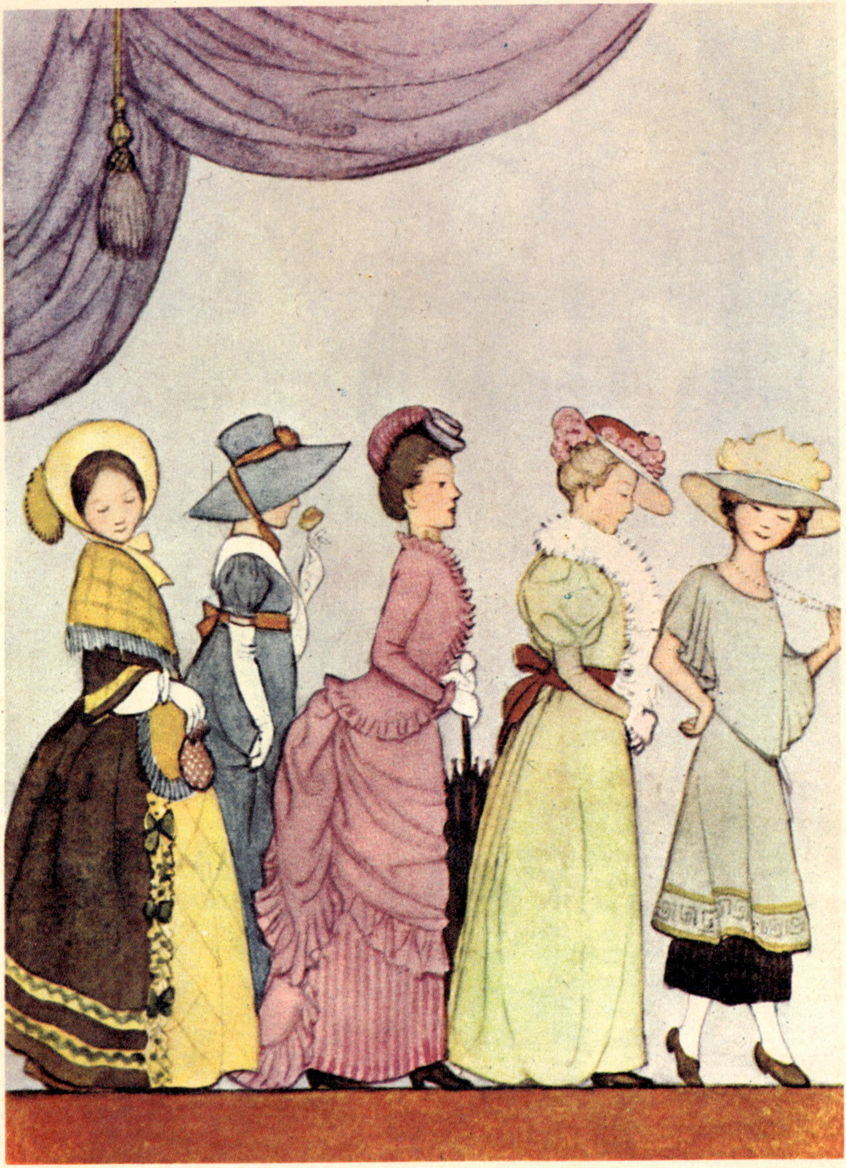

PRINTED BY proost Turnhout (Belgium)

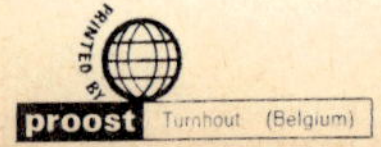

PRINTED IN BELGIUM